THE ADVENTURES OF FINLEY!

ISBN: 978-1-387-47582-7

What a
beautiful day.

sob, sob ribbet!
sob, sob!

Hello...
Who's there?
Are you ok?
sob, sob!

Go away! Don't hurt me!
I would never hurt you! Please come out.

Whoa!
What kind
of frog
are you!?

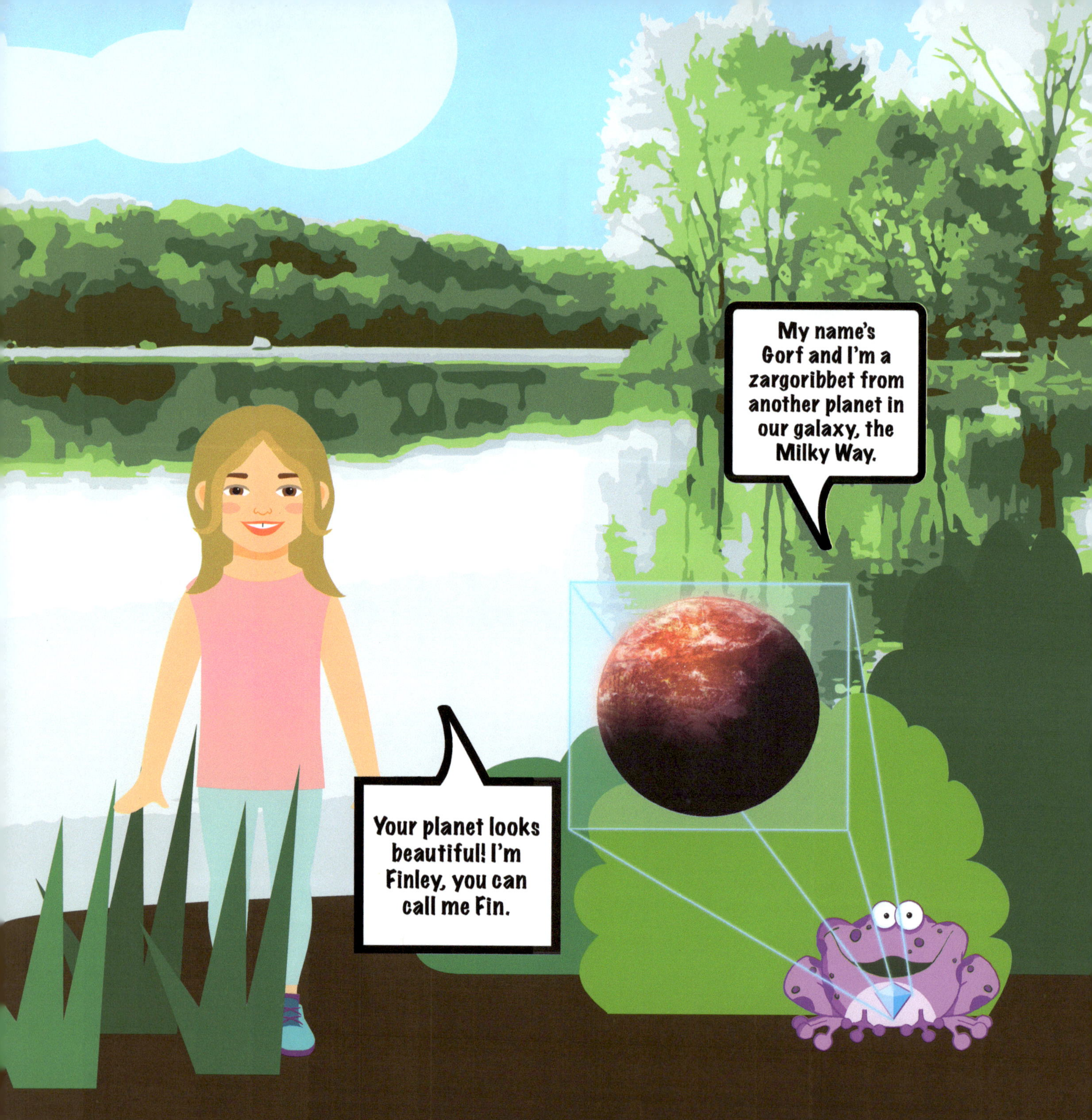
My name's Gorf and I'm a zargoribbet from another planet in our galaxy, the Milky Way.
Your planet looks beautiful! I'm Finley, you can call me Fin.

Thank you Fin.
I crashed my ship while landing earlier today and now I can't get back to my beautiful home.
Ribbet, sob, sob!

Don't cry Gorf, I'll get you home!
You will?
Yes, I just have to figure out how to build a spaceship! Come on, let's go to my house so I can do some research!

FINLEY'S HOUSE!

Gorf, you relax while I figure this out!

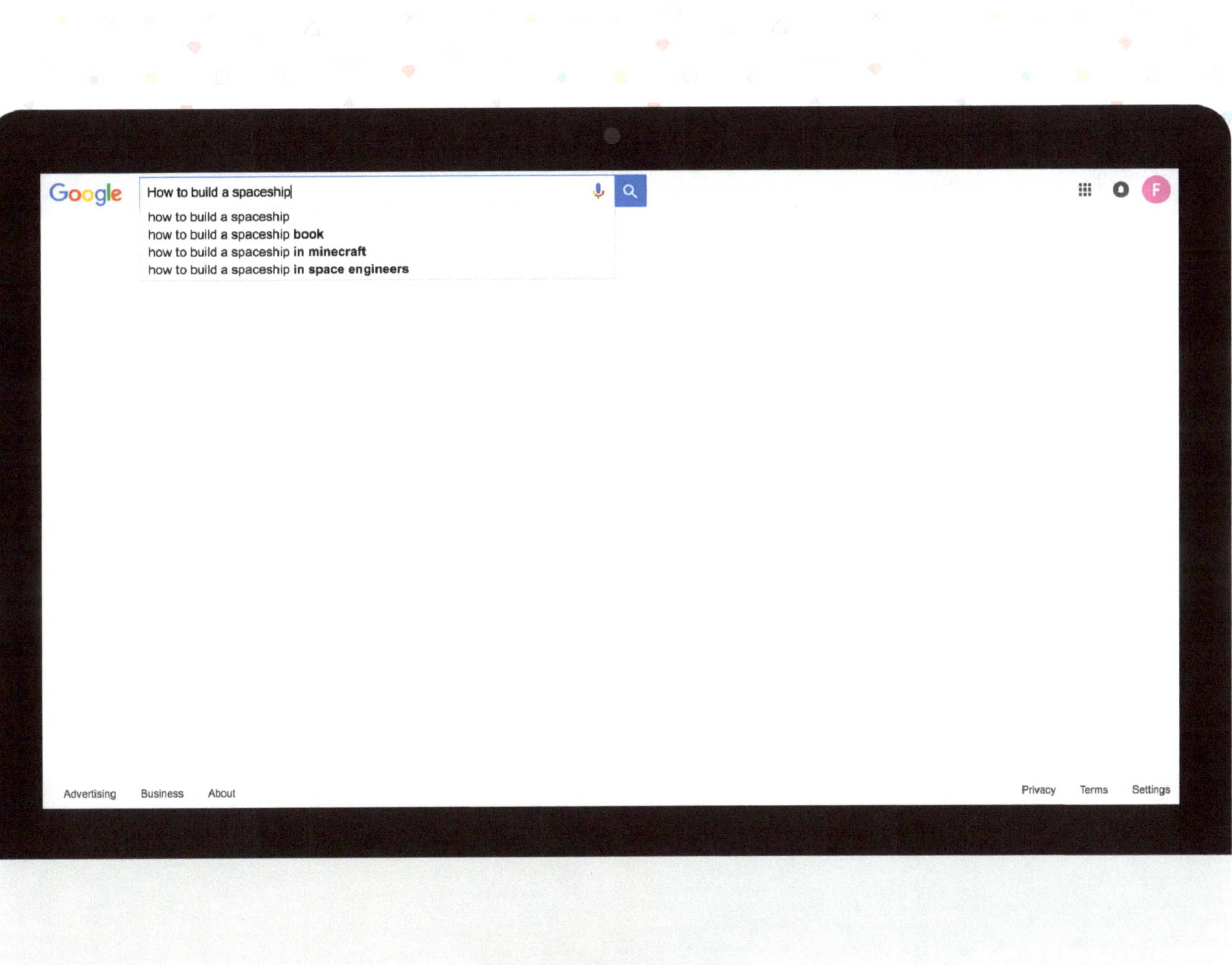
Google
How to build a spaceship
how to build a spaceship
how to build a spaceship book
how to build a spaceship in minecraft
how to build a spaceship in space engineers
F
Advertising
Business
About
Privacy
Terms
Settings

Jackpot!
Time to collect supplies!

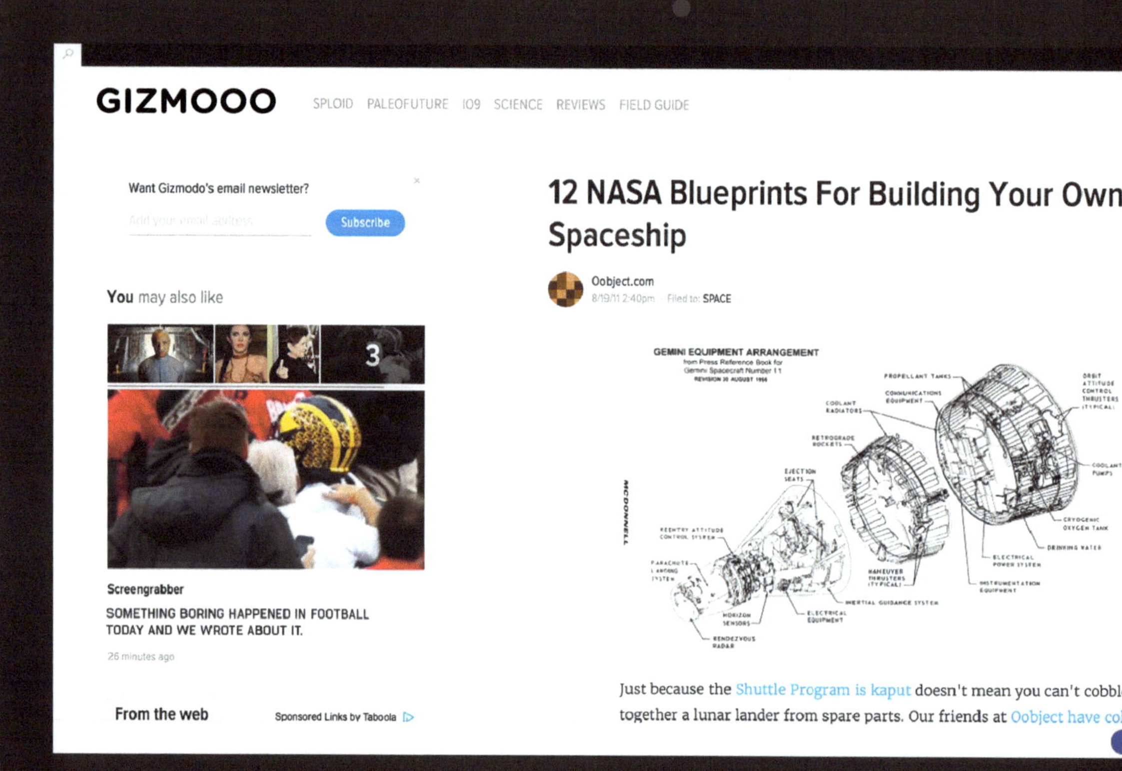

FIND SUPPLIES!

I know there's good stuff in here...
Peeeeee-uuuuuuuu!

Good find Fin!
Look at this!!!

I think I have everything I need. Now it's time for the fun part!

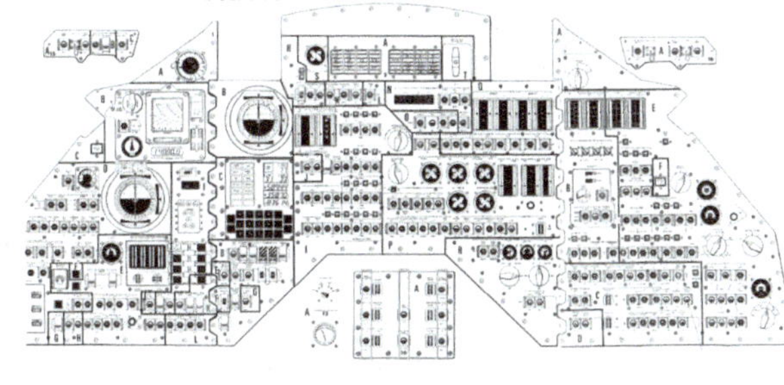

TIME TO BUILD!

APOLLO COMMAND MODULE MAIN CONTROL PANEL
Fin, there's so many parts, how are you going to build the ship!?
Easy! I go step by step.

Step 1: lay out my parts in order.
LIGHT SPEED

Step 2, assemble the ship.

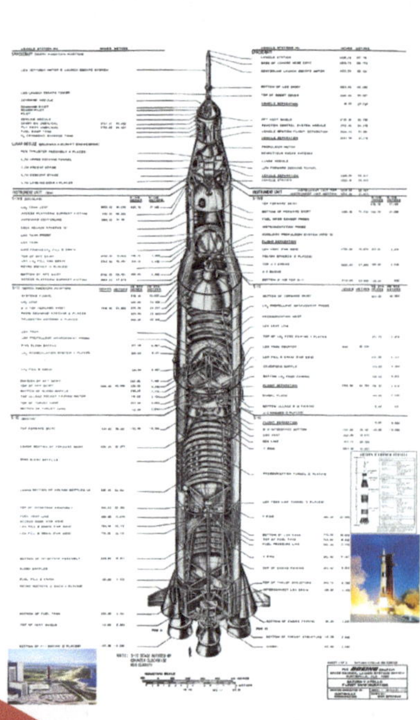

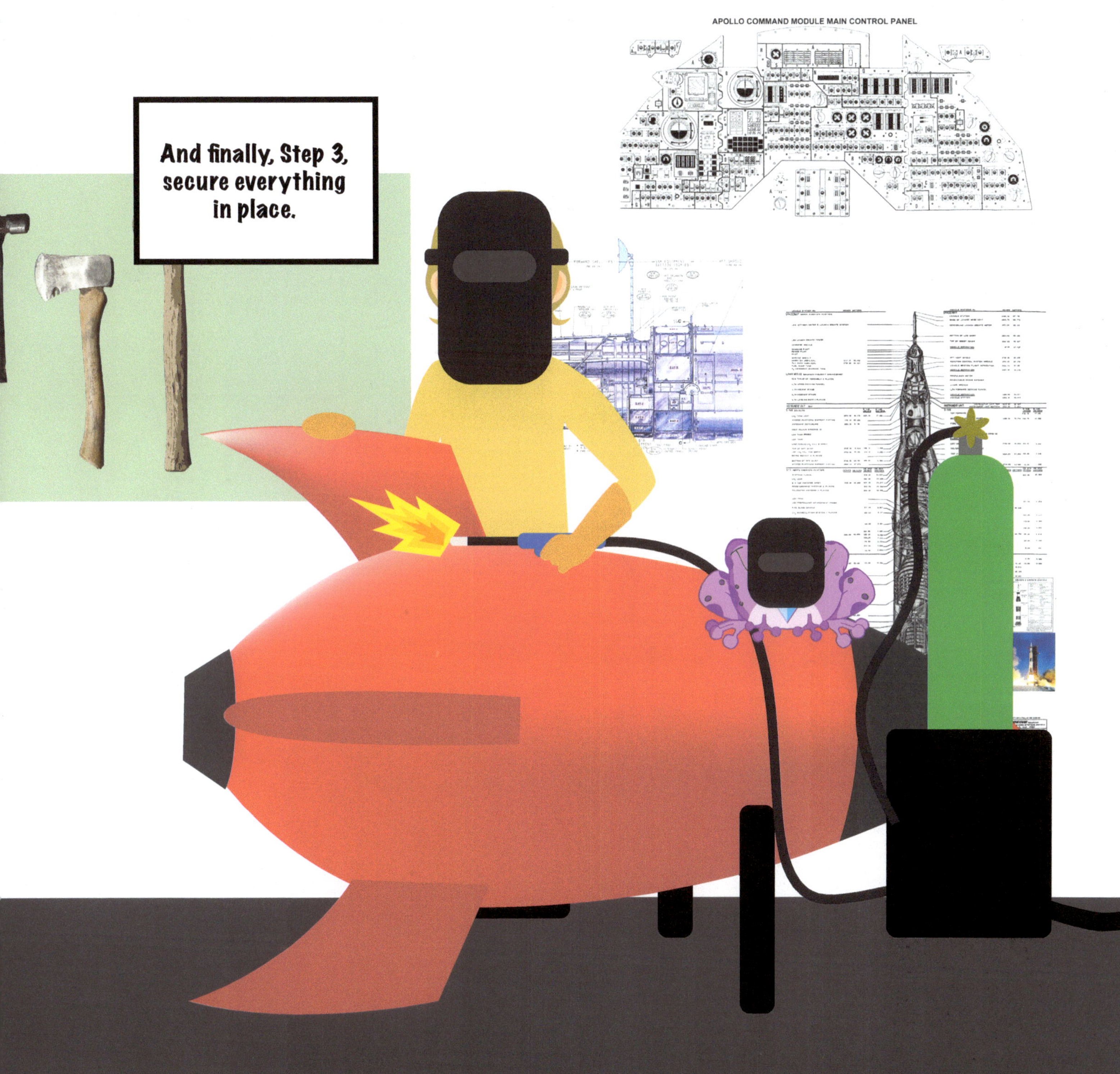
APOLLO COMMAND MODULE MAIN CONTROL PANEL
And finally, Step 3, secure everything in place.

APOLLO COMMAND MODULE MAIN CONTROL PANEL
You did it!
That's right! Now lets get you home!

UP IN SPACE!

Weeeee
eeeee!

Wooooooo
ooooo!

Gorf, enter the coordinates for your home planet.
Ok!

The coordinates are in!
Good, now let's go lightspeed!

LIGHT
SPEED

There it is! There's home!
Hop into the spacepod, it can take you straight from the ship to your planet.

I will,
I promise!
Bye Gorf!
I'll miss you!

Thank you Finley! Promise to visit me soon!

I better get home. Time for.....

LIGHT

SPEED

THE END

www.ingramcontent.com/pod-product-compliance
Lightning Source LLC
LaVergne TN
LVHW070157110826
845147LV00002B/433

* 9 7 8 1 3 8 7 4 7 5 8 2 7 *